A Parrot's Healthy
MEAL PLANNER

Easy recipes to help you feed your bird
a balanced nutritional diet, Book 1

KARMEN BUDAI

All rights reserved. No part of this publication may be reproduced in any form or by means such as printing, photocopying, scanning without prior written permission of the copyright holder. Every effort has been made to ensure that the information in this book is accurate and complete at the time of first publishing. This book has been created solely for motivation and information purposes and must not replace or override professional medical advice.

For permissions contact: info@pollysnaturalparrotboutique.com
www.pollysnaturalparrotboutique.com

Publisher: K&S Natural Company Ltd, 71-75 Shelton Street
Covent Garden, London WC2H 9JQ, United Kingdom

Text copyright © 2020 Karmen Budai, K&S Natural Company Ltd
Additional articles contributed by Dr Stephanie Lamb, DVM
Cover, layout and design by Goldust Design
Food photography by Karmen Budai
Editor: Wendy Janes

ISBN-978-1-5272-5938-6

CONTENTS

Foreword 4

INTRODUCTION 5
The Importance of a Diverse Diet 6
Feeding the Fussy Eater 9
The Benefits of Herbal Teas for Parrots 12
Why I Chose Tea for My Birds 14
The Dirty Dozen 17
The Myths about Sprouts 18
Prep Before Making the Meals 19

RECIPES 21
Your Parrot's Weekly Meal Recipes 23
Vegetable Smoothies 47

Shopping List 49
About the Author 52
About the Contributor 53
Resources 54

FOREWORD

Hello, parrot lovers!

In recent years avian nutrition has become my big passion and I have dedicated a significant amount of my time researching and educating myself about avian nutrition from the best and fully qualified experts in the avian field. What set me off on this journey was my Lesser Sulphur-Crested Cockatoo, Polly, and her battle with a series of unexpected health issues. Since then I have turned this passion into a purpose to advocate and inspire other parrot owners to transition their flock onto fresh foods and point out how diet plays a crucial role in birds' lives. This resulted in the publishing of my very first cookbook in 2018, when *A Parrot's Fine Cuisine Cookbook and Nutritional Guide* was born.

My passion for parrots and their wellbeing didn't stop there, and the opening of an online store for avian organic herbal tea provision was just another way of providing enrichment and diversity in birds' diet to help them lead better lives.

I truly hope that this parrot meal planner can help transform the way you think and feed your birds and will spark your culinary creativity. Most of these recipes are simple enough for any new parrot owner but exciting enough to wow your feathered companion. Every bird can be transitioned onto fresh food, but it will need your patience, persistence and good timing to decide when and how to offer the food. The article from our avian specialist veterinarian Dr Lamb "Feeding the Fussy Eater" provides detailed advice about this transition.

Wishing you and your feathered companion many happy and healthy meals.

Karmen Budai and Polly

Introduction

THE IMPORTANCE OF A DIVERSE DIET

Feeding your bird a healthy balanced diet is not always the easiest task. The lack of scientific studies on parrot nutrition and the contradictory information you find on the internet and social media these days can be a bit confusing at times.

The common question remains though: What diet is right for our precious birds? In the wild, parrots' dietary requirements are always adapted to what's available in their natural habitat and vary considerably depending on the season. Their diet consists mainly of vegetables, fruit, seeds, nuts, insects, buds, flowers and other plant material, plus drinking water from puddles that are brimming with many fallen plants and flowers. However, in captivity it's a whole different story.

Back in the old days when parrot owners fed their birds an exclusive seeded diet they thought it would be enough to satisfy their nutritional needs. This has proven to be wrong and caused all sorts of nutritional deficiencies leading to some serious health problems. Birds were vitamin A deficient, their feather quality was poor, and their immune system weakened. Unfortunately, many parrots, even nowadays, are still not fed a nutritionally balanced diet, which is either due to a lack of understanding by their carers about the implications poor diet can have on their pet bird, or due to a lack of information available to them. Imagine if you had to eat the same type of food every day all day long for the rest of your life. Firstly, how boring would that be, right? Secondly, how would your body react to such an extreme diet and what health problems would that bring over time? Seeds are a great addition in your bird's diet as long as it is not the ONLY food they eat, so keep that in mind. Popular theories on birds' nutrition that applied years ago are no longer relevant these days.

It is important for us "parronts" to educate ourselves and try to offer a diverse diet to our birds so they can live a happy, healthy life. Don't be afraid of experimenting and offering fresh food with sprouted or soaked seeds, legumes, fresh herbs, tree nuts or edible flowers. Colourful bowls packed with a variety of vegetables will always attract the inquisitive bird. It is recommended you mix as many different colours as possible, as each colour of vegetable usually contains different essential vitamins your bird needs. There's so much out there we can offer to enrich their meals. Our birds need all the nutrients to keep them healthy and what better way to satisfy their needs than by offering them what nature offers us.

Fresh chops or mashes are a great way to start, and they are easy to make. Many parrots living in captivity have never been lucky enough to eat a healthy diet, but they can always be introduced to it. It's never too late to make that important change, and offering only one or two of the same pieces of vegetables daily won't do the trick. A well-balanced diet will improve the quality of the feathers, behaviour and overall happiness of your pet bird and my flock is the perfect example that it truly works. Food choices work both ways: a poor diet can cause illness and a good diet can cure illness.

I see that parrots' diet is still one of the most popular topics discussed on social media where parrot owners often discuss their struggles with what to feed their pet, what's not parrot appropriate food, when is the best time to introduce new food, how to wean them off the exclusive seeded diet, not to mention dealing with some seriously fussy beaks where the carer eventually gives up after seeing the bird won't touch any of the offered vegetables.

Remember, persistence is key. Transition for some birds can take months, if not longer, and it is essential to continue trying and offering the food in a form that will grab their attention, but that doesn't mean a bowl of colourful

pellets will satisfy their nutritional needs. Do you really know what is in the pellets you offer to your bird? I always say, read the packaging labels because a label will tell you exactly what your bird will be getting for their breakfast, lunch and dinner. If it sounds more like a chemical soup or if it contains fillers such as peanuts, soy or corn, any colourants, preservatives, sugar and synthetic vitamins, perhaps reconsider whether this is really what you want your bird to eat. Plus, pellets should never be considered as the complete diet and if offered shouldn't form more than 10% of your bird's diet. Ultimately, our goal is to offer diverse raw whole food which will give them access to all the nutrients they need and in the most natural form. Fuel their body with real food not processed food.

In the wild, birds fly off in search of their first meal at daybreak so it's very important to include their most nutritious meal first thing in the morning when they are at their hungriest. The early afternoon hours are usually spent preening, playing, napping and bathing. Afterwards, they feed again, then return to their home for the night.

As their caregivers, we must fit their feedings around our schedules, but try to focus on the two most nutritional meals in the day – breakfast and dinner.

Parrots are highly intelligent birds and foraging can be another way of either introducing new food to them or keeping their minds occupied. Get creative and try hanging vegetables onto parrot-safe stainless-steel skewers or from the side of the cage so they can forage on them. Let them work for their food in the same way they would do it in the wild, as lack of activity can then lead

to boredom which then results in behavioural issues such as feather plucking, which is a whole new issue you want to avoid.

Lastly, whether you are transitioning your bird onto raw whole foods or you simply want to improve their diet, always remember presentation plays an important part. Birds love vibrant colours, so the more colourful and visually appealing the meal, the better chance you have in succeeding.

Remember the old saying "You are what you eat" also applies to our feathered friends too!

FEEDING THE FUSSY EATER

Dr Stephanie Lamb, DVM, Dipl ABVP

Parrots are cautious by nature. Living in the wild can be a dangerous feat and in order to survive they must be smart about their environment and deliberate about everything they encounter until it is known to be safe. Dangers in our homes are a far stretch from the perils that a bird would encounter in the wild; however, their cautious nature remains. After all, parrots are not domesticated as our dogs and cats are, which means they have far more instinctual behaviours that guide their actions.

Birds' guarded behaviour is seen in their attitudes towards food. New items are often approach warily and may not be explored at all by a parrot. How do we get our birds to try new foods then? There are many tricks and tips that owners should try. What works well for one parrot may not for another so don't be discouraged! Just try different routes and one will eventually work for your bird.

Reduce the volume of food

One of the most common mistakes I see people make with their birds is overfeeding. They may be feeding a great diet full of nutritious items, but too much food allows a bird to be selective, and the fact is, birds will pick out what tastes good, not necessarily what is most nutritious.

Therefore, if you are trying to get your bird to eat a new food item, offer only the caloric amount a bird needs per day and the bird will be more likely to try that new item once it gets hungry.

The amount a bird needs to eat varies based on the species, age, level of activity and health status. The best way to know how much to feed your bird is to consult with your avian veterinarian and have your bird's daily caloric needs calculated. However, a few general ideas about volumes of food to feed are as follows: a bird the size of a budgerigar will get about 2 tsp, a conure about 1 tbsp, an African grey approximately 2–2.5 tbsp, and a macaw 5 tbsp.

Pretend you are enjoying the food

Birds, like people, are social creatures and learn what they should eat based on seeing what others consume. If a bird is human bonded, then sitting down together at supper time and sharing a meal is a great way to show your bird what is safe to eat. First, have the bird sit on the back of a chair at the dinner table or place it directly on the table. Then bring out the foods you want your bird to try. Start playing with the food items by picking them up one by one. Explore them with your fingers by turning them around and bring them up to your lips. Pretend you are eating the food or take a bite out of it yourself.

Act excited by the food. Blink your eyes rapidly. This can be interpreted by a bird as you "flashing" your pupils in excitement, just as they will do when they are enjoying a food item. Make lots of vocalizations that indicate pleasure. A loud, "Mmmm," or, "That is so good," can make a bird understand what you have is worthwhile trying. Hand the food to the bird and see what they do next!

One important thing to keep in mind with this tactic is that if you are eating something the bird should not have, be mindful and eat that item away from the bird. If getting it to taste and explore new foods by sharing items together works, you won't want to tease your bird by not giving it something that it shouldn't be eating.

Have a friend bird teach your bird how to eat different foods

Along the same lines, having a bird that is social with other birds, may require a similar but slightly different approach. If you have one parrot who is good at eating certain food items, have that bird interact with the fussy eater. Let them be together and put out the item you want them to eat. Do not provide any other items during this time. As the fussy eater watches the more adventurous eater snack on the food, they may start to realize the item is safe for them to try too.

Offer new food first thing in the morning

One old trick that people have used for many years is feeding the bird the new food at the time of day when it is most hungry. Since most birds do not consume midnight snacks they will have a nearly empty gastrointestinal tract in the morning and thus will be hungry and ready to eat. If the new food you want the bird to try is offered and is the only thing available then the bird is going to have to make a decision. Eat or go hungry for a few hours. If the bird does not try the new food within a few hours, foods that the owner knows the bird will eat should be given. Most birds will at least start to pick the food up and play with it a little, especially as they see the item more and more. It may take several days of trying out this method before the bird chooses to eat the new food. Therefore, patience is required for this technique.

Chop

Chop is a great way to sneak healthy foods and more variety into a diet. This tactic involves taking a variety of fresh foods and cutting them up into tiny pieces then mixing them all together. If done correctly the items are small and it becomes hard for the bird to pick out the things it likes over the things it doesn't like. There are many varieties of chop, and depending upon which ingredients are added to a mix a bird may be more or less excited about this dining option. If one variety of chop is not well accepted, try to change out a few ingredients or reduce the amounts of certain ones and see if the bird likes another variety better. If there is a particular food item you really want your bird to have but the bird is not interested, then start by adding this ingredient to the chop in very small quantities and gradually increase the amount.

Conclusion

Getting a bird to try new food items can sometimes be challenging but it is not impossible. Often it is more a function of an owner not trying hard enough as opposed to the bird truly being a fussy eater. Birds are great at training their owners to give them what they want but that is not always what is most healthy. Therefore, being strict and working with one of the above techniques can get a fussy bird to try something new.

THE BENEFITS OF HERBAL TEAS FOR PARROTS

Dr Stephanie Lamb, DVM, Dipl ABVP

Tea is a popular drink touted to have many health benefits for people, but did you know that you can use it for your bird too? Teas are made from different plant components that have been steeped in hot water to bring out the chemicals within. These then can have effects on the body when an individual drink the tea. There is very little known about the health benefits of teas specifically in birds; however, veterinarians have successfully used teas in various species to treat different problems.

One of the most well-accepted teas for use in medical disorders is the use of black tea in the treatment of iron storage disease. Iron storage disease is a problem where there is an excessive amount of iron that gets stored in the body and can cause damage to the liver and other organs. Black tea has a compound in it known as tannin. Tannins help reduce the absorption of iron from the gastrointestinal tract. Therefore, when black tea is

added to the diet of a patient that has this disease, they will absorb less iron from the foods they eat, which helps to reduce the damaging effects of excess iron being stored in the body.[1]

Another example of the use of tea to improve a bird's health is chamomile. It has been used most commonly for its calming effects though it may have other health benefits as well. When it comes to using this tea for calming, birds have been known to be given this before stressful events such as trips to the vet or to the groomers. It has been recommended for use for anxious birds or feather pluckers. As for its other health benefits, chamomile does have some antioxidant properties due to the flavones it contains.[2] Although not studied yet in pet birds, in humans it can cause a reduction in lipids in the blood. This may be a benefit for birds as well since high lipids in the blood is a commonly identified problem.

Green tea powder has been studied in chickens. In these birds it has been found to reduce oxidative stress on the body, lower cholesterol and triglyceride levels in the blood as well as lower levels of cholesterol and fat in the liver.[3,4,5] In these studies it was fed as 0.5–2% of the diet. Studies like this have not been performed on pet parrots. Pet parrots frequently present to veterinarians for disorders like fatty liver syndrome, atherosclerosis, egg yolk strokes and lipomas, all of which are associated with high fat levels. It should be kept in mind that there is caffeine in green tea powder so consulting with your avian veterinarian is recommended before using this as caffeine may not be appropriate for a bird. Additionally, in chickens when green tea is added to the diet it will reduce the amounts of a common parasite called coccidia.[6] Until further studies are performed on pet parrots we can only speculate.

Other ingredients in teas may be of benefit as well. Raspberry leaf may reduce hormonal problems. Dandelion leaf could help with liver disease. Ginger root may reduce oxidative stress to cells. Teas have the potential to be of great benefit and further studies are desperately needed on birds to help us unlock the healing potential they may possess.

References

1. Seibels, B., Lamberski, N., Gregory, C.R., Slifka, K. and Hagerman, A.E. Effective use of tea to limit dietary iron available to starlings (*Sturnus vulgaris*). *Journal of Zoo and Wildlife Medicine*. 2003; 34: 314–316.
2. Rafraf, M., Zemestani, M. and Asghari-Jafarabadi, M. Effectiveness of chamomile tea on glycemic control and serum lipid profile in patients with type 2 diabetes. *Journal of Endocrinological Investigation*. 2015; 38: 163–170.
3. Eid, Y.Z., Ohtsuka, A., Hayashi, K. Tea polyphenols reduce glucocorticoid induced growth inhibition and oxidative stress in broiler chickens. *British Poultry Science*. 2003; 44: 127–132.
4. Afsharmanesh, M. and Sadaghi, B. Effects of dietary alternative (probiotic, green tea powder, and Kombucha tea) as antimicrobial growth promoters on growth, ileal nutrient digestibility, blood parameters, and immune response of broiler chickens. *Comparative Clinical Pathology*. 2014; 23: 717–724.
5. Biswas, A. and Wakita, M. Effect of dietary Japanese green tea powder supplementation on feed utilization and carcass profiles in broilers. *Journal of Poultry Science*. 2001; 38: 50–57.
6. Jang, S.I., Jun, M., Lillehoj, H.S., et al. Anti-coccidial effects of green tea-based diets against Eimeria maxima. *Veterinary Parasitology*. 2007; 144: 172–175.

WHY I CHOSE TEA FOR MY BIRDS

Did you know that tea is the second most consumed drink in the world, second only to water? But have you ever thought of offering it to your pet bird? How did we even come around the idea of giving this type of drink to our beloved parrots?

Well, not many people have heard of an avian tea before and even in 2017, I certainly had no idea this was even an option. I stumbled across avian teas when I joined Dr Jason Crean's Facebook group, and began learning all about avian nutrition and how to improve my bird's diet. I was curious to find out more about it and how this could help my bird, especially after going through some rough times with my cockatoo, Polly, when she became seriously ill. When Polly was discharged from the vet and we were finally able to take her home, she still wasn't herself and looked poorly, even after being home for nearly a week she wasn't improving. We feared we would have to take her back to the vet, which would have involved a long drive. Luckily, the tea arrived (just in time) and we started offering it to her twice a day. We soon observed that she had miraculously improved and perked up. By the fourth day she was back to normal and hopping around as if nothing had happened. The tea was a lifesaver.

This experience inspired me to launch Polly's own avian tea range, first in the UK, so other parrots could also benefit from these powerful herbs. I was fortunate in being able to work with Dr Jason Crean, MS Bio, EdD, a biologist, a certified avian specialist and president of The Avicultural Society of Chicagoland in the US; whose valued expertise in avian nutrition has aided us in the understanding of the best-suited dietary and nutritional requirements of parrots like Polly. His ideology is centred around promoting the implementation of a raw whole-food diet for the animals in our care; helping them to not only survive, but to thrive through increasing dietary diversity. This is something I wholeheartedly support, and he is the mastermind behind the development of these unique avian herbal blends that can enrich your bird's quality of life.

What are herbal teas?

Herbal teas, also referred to as herbal infusions (tisanes), are basically the leaves, seeds, fruit or other parts of edible plants. They do not come from the Camellia sinensis plant, which are harvested to produce only caffeinated black, green, oolong and white teas. Each tea has its own unique character and offers something else, so here are some examples of the health benefits[1] these herbs can offer and which we have also included in our avian blends.

Nature Boost Organic Avian Herbal Tea

Golden Blossom Organic Avian Herbal Tea

Eternal Feathers Organic Avian Herbal tea

Chamomile – Known as one of the ancient medicinal herbs for its high level of antioxidants that help fight diseases. It is commonly used because of its calming effects, helping with anxiety and relieving skin irritation thanks to its anti-inflammatory and antibacterial properties. (Key ingredient in our Eternal Feathers blend)

Dandelion leaf – Not many of us know that this plant, which we usually call a weed, is actually loaded with antioxidants, vitamins and minerals and has been used as a natural remedy. It's high in vitamin A, fibre and other vitamins like K and C, possesses antimicrobial properties, acts as a natural diuretic, and helps protect the liver. (Key ingredient in our Golden Blossom and Nature Boost blends)

Milk thistle – The healing properties of milk thistle has been known for centuries. It acts as a natural liver supporter and detoxifier and has been known to work as a filter by removing toxins that are produced through the liver, decreasing or even reversing damage to the liver caused by medications or heavy metals. (Key ingredient in our Golden Blossom blend)

Calendula flower – This beautiful flower has been used for a long time in the cosmetic industry, medicine or simply used in the form of fresh or dried petals in salads. It is known to have strong anti-inflammatory properties, aid in the healing of wounds and it contains antimicrobial and antiviral components. (Key ingredient in our Eternal Feathers blend)

Hibiscus flower – This delicious, deep red tea is mainly known for its ability to lower high blood pressure. It may also help to lower cholesterol and blood sugar. It is packed with antioxidants that fight free radical damage caused by a poor diet. (Key ingredient in our Nature Boost blend)

These herbal teas present the opportunity to go back to basics and focus on wellness in our pets through a holistic approach.

[1] The nutrition facts provided here are based on animal and human studies. Since very little research has been done on birds like parrots compared to that of mammals, we must use what we know and apply that knowledge to the physiology of other species.

THE DIRTY DOZEN

When shopping for fruit and vegetables for your beloved pet bird it is always advisable to consider buying as much organic produce as possible. But we all know this is not always possible for various reasons, and the high price of organic produce doesn't seem to help either. So, what does "dirty dozen" refer to? If you've not heard of this phrase before, it is basically the top 12 fruits and vegetables that are known for being the most likely to be covered in pesticide residue. Of course, we want to keep our birds healthy and safe from all toxins, but we can't just stop offering these products as they're all part of a diverse healthy diet offering different minerals and vitamins. So, what do we do? We clean them first.

Here's how we safely clean such foods, so you don't need to worry about passing any chemicals on to your pet bird. Washing the "dirty dozen" under tap water won't remove the residue, so the best and parrot-safe way of doing it is by soaking each item in vinegar solution. Organic apple cider vinegar (with the mother) is the best one to use.

Simply fill a large bowl or clean sink with cool water and add a ¼ cup of apple cider vinegar and then pour in the fruit and vegetables. Let them soak for about 10 minutes before rinsing everything thoroughly in cool water.

1. Apples
2. Strawberries
3. Pears
4. Grapes
5. Peaches
6. Bell peppers
7. Spinach
8. Nectarines
9. Kale
10. Cherries
11. Hot peppers
12. Celery (leaves preferred)

Tip: Once you've opened the apple cider vinegar bottle it is always recommended you keep it refrigerated.

THE MYTHS ABOUT SPROUTS

Offering sprouts to your pet bird is a great way to give them more nutrition and enrich their diet. With the recent use and influence of social media, we tend to share all sorts of information to help us become better carers for our pet birds, which is great as our birds are complex creatures and there's still so much we can learn and share about them and their diet. But this can also bring challenges in ensuring the reliability of the information shared. The latest myth I came across was "don't feed your bird sprouts or too much of it as it will cause hormonal imbalance".

Unverified information can sometimes cause more damage than good, and your bird could really miss out on these little nutritional powerhouses. That's why we have asked our avian specialist veterinarian Dr Stephanie Lamb, DVM, Dipl ABVP, to explain the truth behind this. Here is her response:

"Sprouts in and of themselves will not cause hormonal changes. They are a great way to provide variation in the diet and other nutrients that would be less bioavailable to the bird if they ate that item in a non-sprouted form. What can be hormone inducing is too many calories or too much fat or moisture in the diet for certain species. So, if someone who sprouts gives an abundance of them and gives too many calories then that could be hormone inducing. Abundance of calories to a bird means they have a lot of resources. And in their mind, a lot of resources means it's a good time to have babies! Also, for some species, like African greys, they can be stimulated by getting moist foods. It doesn't stimulate all birds this way, just some. Moist foods can be thought of like regurgitated food which can make a bird think their owner is regurgitating to them as a gift to indicate they love them so much and want to have babies with them!

Lastly, it's also the way the food is fed. If any owner makes the food and feeds it to their bird with a lot of cuddling and not making them work for it, then that too can make them hormonal.

So, in short, sprouts don't induce hormone changes in and of themselves. It's more the calorie abundance and presentation that do."

Dr Stephanie Lamb

PREP BEFORE MAKING THE MEALS

You will need to prepare the soaked and sprouted grains, seeds, legumes and nuts in advance before making your bird's meals. The guide below will help you with the soaking and sprouting times.

Soaking

Soaking is a simple process where you soak the item in a cool water for certain period of time.

Step 1: Always make sure you wash the item first before leaving it to soak.

Step 2: Place the item in a bowl and cover it with cool water so it is completely submerged in the water. Leave it to soak as long as required.

Step 3: After soaking, rinse well in cool water and strain. Then it's ready to be added into your bird's fresh food.

...AND WHY SHOULD WE SOAK? There are a few reasons why you should include soaked items in your bird's diet. Soaking nuts, seeds, legumes and grains will not only help to remove the "anti-nutrients" like phytic acids and enzyme inhibitors that protect the seed, nut or grain from germination, but will make the essential vitamins and minerals more available and easier for your pet bird to digest.

Tip: *Soaking will increase, if not double, the size of an item, so ensure you put enough water in a bowl. Soak at room temperature. Never use hot water.*

Sprouting

When sprouting the seeds, grains and legumes for your bird you will need to start with the soaking process first before anything can start to sprout.

Day 1: Once you have completed the above soaking process, place the soaked items into a sprouting jar and cover with a mesh lid to allow good air flow. Make sure any excess water can be drained out during the sprouting process.

Day 2: Rinse well under cool water and place the sprouts in a GSE (Grapefruit Seed Extract) water mixture for about 5 minutes then strain without rinsing. Repeat this step daily – morning and evening – until your sprouts are ready. When you see tiny tails coming out, they're ready to be harvested, so rinse one final time and strain thoroughly before serving.

Tip: *Using specific sprouting jars can be the best way for those new to sprouting as it can easily be inverted and propped at an angle to drain any excess water properly during the sprouting, decreasing chances of getting mouldy*

sprouts. GSE helps to deter any microbial growth, rinsing sprouts in only cool water won't do the job.

Storing sprouts and soaked food

Sprouts and soaked food should be transferred into a plastic container, sealed tightly and stored in the refrigerator for up to a maximum of 3 days. Ensure the sprouts have drained completely before storing them. Always check for any sour smell or mould before serving to your pet bird. If unsure dispose immediately, as any off items may cause illness.

Washing the produce

Always ensure you wash all the fruit and vegetables thoroughly before feeding. You may also use the same method recommended for cleaning the "dirty dozen".

Safety Tip: Never sprout or soak any soup type beans as these can't be fed raw to your pet bird. Soup beans contain a compound called lectin which is toxic, and it can only be removed with cooking.

ITEM	SOAK TIME	SPROUT TIME
Grains		
Amaranth	2–4 hours	1–1.5 days
Pearl barley	6–8 hours	N/A
Buckwheat	15 minutes	1–2 days
Field corn	8–14 hours	2+ days
Kamut	8–14 hours	1–1.5 days
Quinoa (white, red, black)	2 hours	1–2 days
Legumes		
Garbanzo beans (chickpea)	12 hours	12 hours
Lentils (brown/green/red)	8 hours	12 hours
Mung beans	1 day	2–5 days
Nuts & Seeds		
Almonds (hulled)	8–12 hours	12 hours
Cashew	2.5 hours	N/A
Walnut (hulled)	4 hours	N/A
Fenugreek seeds	8 hours	2–3 days
Sesame seeds	8 hours	1–2 days
Sunflower seeds	2 hours	2–3 days
Milk thistle seeds	8 hours	2–3 days
Radish seeds	8 hours	2–3 days
Coriander seeds	8 hours	N/A
Broccoli seeds	8 hours	1–2 days

Recipes

YOUR PARROT'S WEEKLY MEAL RECIPES

Now, before you run into the kitchen and start preparing all these super-healthy meals for your flock, let's have a quick recap on the 3 important steps that will help you transition your birds onto the raw whole food.

Mornings

STEP 1
★ Remove any comfort or their usual foods when serving breakfast to avoid your bird eating what they like the most and not eating what you want them to eat.
★ Remember, breakfast is an important meal for your bird to start the day as it will kick-start their metabolism, so make it raw and super nutritious as they would have it in the wild.

STEP 2
★ If you are introducing a fresh chop to your bird for the first time, monitor them for a couple of hours to ensure they've consumed at least some of the offered fresh food.
★ If you notice your bird's beak hasn't touched anything for about 2 to 3 hours, place their usual food back.
★ Repeat daily and be persistent as this can take months and there will be some food wastage. Presentation plays an important part too.

STEP 3
★ Seeds/pellets can be offered and left in their cage once your bird has consumed their super-healthy breakfast and before serving the evening meal.
★ Place the dry food back into your bird's cage for the night too.
★ Never leave any fresh food in your bird's cage overnight as it'll spoil and can potentially cause health problems if consumed.

Let's get into it.

Tips: *Afternoon snacks are optional to offer and should be in small portions adjusted to the size of your bird. Adjust the recipe portions as needed depending on the number of beaks you are feeding. Try to focus on the two most nutritional meals of the day – breakfast and dinner.*

MONDAY

BREAKFAST
Happy Parrot Chop

Vegetables
¼ cup black cabbage, chopped
½ cup pak choi, finely chopped
2 tbsp fennel, finely chopped
2 Brussels sprouts, cut in halves
¼ cup beetroot, diced
2 tbsp butternut squash, grated
¼ cup kohlrabi, small diced
¼ cup red bell pepper, chopped

Dry Items
1 tbsp white hulled sesame seeds
1 tbsp hemp seeds
1 tbsp organic rolled oats (unsweetened)
1 tbsp flaxseeds (linseeds)

Soaked
1 tbsp milk thistle seeds
1 tbsp almonds
1 tbsp cashews

Sprouted
1 tbsp sunflower seeds
1 tbsp chickpeas (garbanzo beans)

Optional Items
1 tbsp red amaranth microgreens
1 tbsp basil microgreens
1 tsp flaxseed oil
Pansy flowers, to garnish

Prepare the soaked and sprouted ingredients in advance. Chop all the vegetables as suggested and place them in your bird's favourite bowl.

Add all the dry, sprouted and soaked items, and toss gently.

Mix in a teaspoon of the flaxseed oil and add the suggested microgreens for more enrichment. Garnish with parrot-safe edible flowers.

Tip: Did you know that flaxseed oil is loaded with healthy omega-3 fatty acids? These are very important fats that are needed for your bird's brain development and can help reduce cholesterol. When buying flaxseed oil, make sure it comes from the refrigerated section. You can also find omega-3 fatty acids in some green leafy vegetables, nuts, especially walnuts, pecans and hazelnuts or some seeds, such as flaxseed (linseed), pumpkin, hemp and chia seeds.

AFTERNOON SNACK
Pick n Mix Nutty Bowl

Offer a selection of organic tree nuts such as hazelnuts, walnuts, macadamia nuts, almonds, Brazil nuts, cashews and pine nuts.

Add dry pumpkin seeds (pepitas), organic coconut flakes (unsweetened), dried blueberries and cranberries, and Polly's avian herbal tea (dry).

Adjust the quantities depending on your bird's size, and for the large beaks some of the nuts may be offered shelled. (Suitable for medium to large parrots)

For small beaks you may offer spray millet, chopped dry pumpkin seeds, coconut flakes, hemp seeds, hulled sesame seeds and finely chopped nuts instead.

Vegetables and Herbs
1 cup pumpkin or any type squash
1 carrot, peeled and grated
1 tbsp sweetcorn, raw or cooked (not from a tin)
1 tbsp fresh coriander, finely chopped

Dry Items
½ tbsp organic coconut flour
1 tsp hemp seeds
1 tsp flaxseeds (linseeds)
1 tsp Brazil nuts, crushed

DINNER
Pumpkin Croquettes

First chop the pumpkin into small cubes, place the cubes into a steamer basket and cover. Remove once tender and let them cool.

Place the cooked pumpkin in a bowl and mash with a fork until smooth and there are no large chunks left. Add grated carrot, raw or cooked sweetcorn, coriander and all the dry items then stir until well combined. Roll the batter into bite-sized balls depending on the size of your bird.

TUESDAY

BREAKFAST
Greek Chop

Vegetables and Herbs
1 cup kale, chopped
¼ cup cauliflower, chopped
1 small carrot, peeled and small diced
1 red chilli pepper, sliced
½ cup broccoli, chopped
4 green beans, chopped
¼ cup courgette (zucchini), chopped
1 sprig of fresh rosemary, chopped

Dry Items
1 tbsp whole rosehips
1 tbsp ground flaxseeds (linseeds)

Soaked
1 tbsp walnuts, crushed
1 tbsp pearl barley
1 tsp amaranth
1 tbsp black quinoa

Optional Items
1 tsp organic raw coconut oil

Prepare the soaked ingredients in advance. Chop all the vegetables as suggested and place them in your bird's favourite bowl.

Add all the dry and soaked items and toss gently. Mix in a teaspoon of the raw coconut oil.

*When adding a coconut oil into the fresh chop there's no need for it to be melted. Coconut oil has low melting point about 76 °F (24 °C).

AFTERNOON SNACK

Use parrot-safe stainless-steel skewers to thread various fruits such as strawberries, kiwi, apple, grapes, papaya, banana, cantaloupe melon onto, placing a single piece of fruit at a time. Hang it inside your parrot's cage. This is a great foraging exercise and snack at the same time.

Safety Tip: Ensure you purchase a genuine stainless-steel skewer. Non stainless steel or one with a plated coating is not safe as it can flake or rust, and you are risking your bird getting metal poisoning. It is always recommended to buy equipment from a reputable store.

Vegetables
3 sprigs of purple sprouting broccoli, chopped
1 carrot, shredded
1 small green pepper, chopped
4 green beans, chopped
¼ cup cucumber, chopped
1 slice of butternut squash, chopped
2 red and green chilli peppers, sliced, to garnish

¼ cup of chickpeas

Soaked
1 tbsp yellow split peas
1 tbsp red lentils
1 tbsp black sesame seeds

Sprouted
1 tbsp chickpeas (garbanzo beans)
2 tbsp radish seeds

DINNER
Moroccan Spicy Chop

First cook the ¼ cup of chickpeas until tender enough to break up easily. Drain out the cooking liquid and let it cool. Then blend roughly for a couple of seconds in a food processor, just enough to break it up but do not create a paste.

Have the soaked and sprouted items ready prior to making the meal. Chop all the vegetables as suggested and place them into your bird's bowl.

Add all the soaked and sprouted items, followed by the blended chickpeas and toss gently.

Garnish with red and green chilli peppers.

WEDNESDAY

BREAKFAST
Parrot's Chinese Chop

Vegetables and Herbs
1 cup broccoli, chopped
4 Brussels sprouts, sliced
¼ cup Swiss chard, thinly sliced
1 carrot, peeled and shredded
¼ red bell pepper, thinly sliced
¼ orange bell pepper, thinly sliced
4 green beans, chopped
4 sugar snap peas, whole
1 red chilli pepper, sliced
1 sprig of fresh curly parsley, finely chopped
Handful of red mustard microgreens, to garnish

Dry Items
1 tbsp cashews, crushed
1 tbsp white hulled sesame seeds
1 tsp pumpkin seeds (pepitas)
1 tbsp Polly's avian herbal tea – Golden Blossom

Soaked
1 tbsp black sesame seeds

Sprouted
1 tbsp green lentils
1 tbsp mung beans
1 tbsp radish seeds

Prepare the soaked and sprouted ingredients in advance. Chop all the vegetables as suggested and place them into a bowl.

Add the soaked black sesame seeds and the sprouted ingredients, followed by the dry items, including the avian herbal tea, and mix well.

Garnish with red mustard microgreens.

AFTERNOON SNACK
Parrot Pancake with A Twist

Peel the banana and break it up into several big chunks in a bowl. Use a dinner fork to thoroughly mash the banana. Continue mashing until the banana has a pudding-like consistency. Combine with barley flour and egg then add in hemp and chia seeds, rolled oats and mix it well.

Heat a lightly oiled frying pan over a very low heat. Drop roughly a couple of teaspoons of batter onto the hot pan. (Remember, still on low heat.) Cook the pancakes until the bottoms look golden when you lift a corner. The edges should also be starting to look set. Flip the pancakes. Gently work a spatula about halfway under the pancake, then lift until the unsupported half of the pancake is just barely lifted off the skillet. Lay the pancake back down on its other side.

Cook the pancake for another minute or so, until the other side is also light gold. You can flip the pancakes a few times if you need to in order to get them evenly browned and thoroughly cooked. Transfer the cooked pancakes to a serving plate or bowl and place a slice of steamed green plantain on top. To help hold the slice of plantain, pierce it all the way through with a bamboo skewer. Garnish with live waxworms or mealworms. Mini pancakes can be frozen in single batches and defrosted when required (except the mealworms).

Safety Tip: Only raw coconut oil is recommended for parrots and no other cooking oils should be used!

Nutrition Tip: Waxworms or mealworms are great source of protein which is an essential component of a bird's balanced diet. It supports tissue repair, growth of muscle and skin, feather growth, hormone production, immune system and energy. But as with everything, all in moderation as too much protein in your bird's diet has been linked to the development of lipogranulomas in the liver.

½ banana
1 organic egg
½ cup barley flour
1 tsp hemp seeds
1 tsp chia seeds
1 tbsp organic rolled oats (unsweetened)
Slices of green plantain, steamed
1 tsp organic raw coconut oil
1 small bamboo skewer
1 tsp live waxworms or mealworms, to garnish

DINNER
Polly's Muesli Bowl

Fruit and Vegetables
1 tbsp blueberries, whole
¼ cup honeydew melon, diced
½ carrot, peeled and grated
1 tbsp blackberries, cut in half
¼ red apple, grated
1 green plum, chopped
1 tbsp pomegranate seeds

Dry Items
1 tbsp chia seeds
1 tbsp barley flakes
1 tbsp organic coconut flakes (unsweetened), to garnish

Soaked
1 tbsp cashews, chopped

Optional Items
1 edible pansy flower, to garnish

Soak the cashews the day before making the meal. Chop all the fruit as suggested, add grated carrot and place it all in a bowl.

Start adding all the dry items followed by the chopped cashews and pomegranate seeds, gently mix. Sprinkle with coconut flakes.

An edible pansy flower will always make the food look more desirable even to those fussy beaks.

Safety Tip: When buying flowers, ensure they are listed as edible, organically grown and suitable for human consumption, unless you are growing your own. Flowers from garden centres, nurseries and florists are designed to be looked at, not eaten. They are sprayed with insecticides and fungicides which are not safe for your bird. Always ensure that the flower is on a safe bird food list.

THURSDAY

BREAKFAST
Calcium Booster

Vegetables
1 cup of kale, chopped
¼ cup marrow squash, chopped
¼ cup green beans, chopped
2 okras, sliced
½ cup purple sprouting broccoli, chopped
1 carrot, peeled and grated
½ red bell pepper, chopped
1 tbsp raw sweetcorn
1 tbsp turnip, grated

Dry Items
1 tsp pine nuts
1 tbsp hazelnuts
1 tbsp macadamia nuts, roughly chopped
1 tbsp Polly's avian herbal tea – Golden Blossom

Sprouted
1 tbsp green lentils
1 tbsp mung beans

Optional Items
1 tbsp cabbage microgreens
1 tbsp beet microgreens

First prepare your sprouted green lentils and mung beans in advance. Chop all the vegetables as suggested.

Combine the dry items, sprouted lentils, mung beans, microgreens and chopped vegetables in a bowl and toss gently.

AFTERNOON SNACK
Fruity Bowl

Fruit and Herbs
4 strawberries, chopped
1 tbsp pomegranate seeds
¼ cup watermelon, diced
¼ red apple, peeled, grated into chips
¼ cup honeydew melon, including seeds
1 sprig of fresh mint, finely chopped

Dry Items
1 tbsp almond flakes
1 tbsp Brazil nuts, chopped
Pinch of Ceylon cinnamon

Chop all the fruit as suggested and place into a bowl. Add finely chopped fresh mint, followed by the dry items, including the pinch of Ceylon cinnamon. Mix and serve.

Safety Tip: When including cinnamon in your bird's diet it is important to know which one is safe for your precious companion. Never use Cassia cinnamon, only the true Ceylon cinnamon is safe for our birds.

DINNER
Green Foraging Flower

Vegetables
2 small baby peppers, chopped
¼ cup courgette (zucchini), diced
Handful of baby spinach, whole
¼ cup butternut squash, diced
¼ cup white chicory, thinly sliced
1 tbsp kohlrabi, diced
1 tbsp cress microgreens, to garnish
2 whole leaves of savoy cabbage, as serving platter

2 tbsp red quinoa, cooked

Dry Items
1 tbsp Polly's avian herbal tea – Nature Boost

Soaked
1 tbsp almonds

Sprouted
2 tbsp buckwheat

First prepare your soaked and sprouted ingredients in advance. To cook quinoa, rinse it first under cold running water. Put it in a pan with water over a medium heat and bring to the boil. Reduce to a simmer for 10 to 15 minutes, or until tender and the liquid is absorbed. Once cooked, drain any excess water and let it cool down. Chop all the vegetables as suggested. In a bowl, mix all the chopped vegetables with the cooked quinoa, soaked almonds, sprouted buckwheat and avian herbal tea.

Place the two whole savoy cabbage leaves onto a plate on top of each other then start placing whole spinach leaves around on top. Place the veggie mixture onto the savoy cabbage leaves and garnish with cress microgreens.

BREAKFAST
Rio's Mash

Vegetables and Herbs
¼ cup kale, chopped
½ each yellow and green bell peppers, chopped
4 small radishes, finely chopped
¼ cup cauliflower, chopped
1 sprig of fresh curly parsley, finely chopped
4 sugar snap peas, chopped
1 carrot, peeled and grated
1 red chilli pepper, chopped and sliced, to garnish
Beetroot, sliced, to garnish

Dry Items
1 tbsp barley flakes

Soaked
1 tbsp pearl barley
1 tbsp coriander seeds
1 tbsp green lentils

Sprouted
1 tbsp mung beans
1 tbsp milk thistle seeds

Optional Items
1 tbsp Polly's avian herbal tea – Nature Boost

Prepare the soaked and sprouted ingredients in advance. Chop all the vegetables as suggested and place them in your bird's favourite bowl.

Add barley flakes, avian herbal tea, sprouts and soaked items, toss gently. Garnish with a couple of slices of beetroot and chilli peppers.

AFTERNOON SNACK
Stuffed Foraging Apple

1 large or medium-sized red apple (peeled if not organic)

Dried Items
1–2 tbsp of your bird's seed mix

First, cut off a thin slice from the top where you start coring the apple. Then insert a tablespoon and give it a twist and scoop out the core carefully. Core it about ¾ of the way down so that when stuffing the apple, the seeds won't fall out from the bottom.

Once cored, stuff the apple with your bird's favourite seed mix. Serve the whole apple in their bowl or simply hang it onto the stainless-steel skewer.

You may cover the apple with the previously cut top to create more excitement when your bird is searching for those favourite seeds. This is a great and messy foraging "treat" with plenty to eat and it keeps your bird occupied too.

---

1 tbsp organic brown rice, cooked
1 tbsp raw peas
1 carrot, peeled and sliced
1 tbsp courgette (zucchini), chopped
1 chilli pepper, to garnish

Soaked
1 tbsp fenugreek seeds
1 tbsp kamut
1 tsp radish seeds

Sprouted
1 tbsp buckwheat

DINNER
Quick Fix

Prepare the soaked and sprouted ingredients in advance. Then, combine the brown rice with some water in a pot and bring to the boil. Reduce heat, cover and simmer until tender.

Cool the rice in cold water right after cooking and drain.

Place all the ingredients in your bird's favourite bowl and mix well, garnish with chilli pepper.

SATURDAY

BREAKFAST
Purple Chop

Vegetables and Herbs
¼ cup savoy cabbage, finely chopped
1 carrot, finely chopped
¼ cup buttonhole kale (purple), finely chopped
¼ cup broccoli, chopped
5 green beans, chopped
½ of white chicory, sliced
4 okra, sliced
½ cup yellow and red bell peppers, chopped
1 tbsp fresh oregano, finely chopped
1 sprig fresh dill, chopped
2 bird's eye chillies, chopped
2 baby sweetcorn, sliced
¼ cup pumpkin, chopped (with seeds)
Handful of lamb's lettuces, as serving platter
Cress microgreens, to garnish

Dry Items
1 tbsp organic rolled oats (unsweetened)
1 tbsp shelled hemp seeds
1 tsp ground flaxseeds (linseeds)
1 tbsp pecan nuts, crushed
1 tbsp Polly's avian herbal tea – Nature Boost

Sprouted
1 tbsp corn (optional) – for medium and large birds only
1 tbsp milk thistle seeds

Prepare the sprouted ingredients in advance. Chop all the vegetables and herbs as suggested and place them in a bowl.

Add all the dry and sprouted items, and toss gently.

Fill the bottom of a bowl with lamb's lettuce and place the vegetable mixture on top and garnish with cress microgreens.

Nutrition Tip: Fresh or dried oregano is not only nutritionally beneficial to your bird, but it will also help to preserve and prolong the freshness of the raw whole foods as well as deter any microbial growth. Oregano contains an essential compound called carvacrol, which has antimicrobial properties. Saying that, it doesn't mean that keeping your bird's chop out all day and night will keep it fresh and safe to eat.

2 tbsp sweet potato
¼ ripe banana
1 tbsp pumpkin seeds (pepitas), chopped
1 tsp shelled hemp seeds
1 tbsp white hulled sesame seeds

Dry Mix
1 tbsp almonds, walnuts, crushed
1 tbsp organic coconut flour

AFTERNOON SNACK
Parrot Truffles

Peel and cut the sweet potato into small cubes, place them into a steamer basket, and cover. Remove from steamer when tender and let it cool. Mash the sweet potato and ripe banana with a fork, then add chopped pumpkin seeds, shelled hemp and sesame seeds, mix well.

Form small truffles size of 3 cm/1 inch in diameter then roll and coat them individually in the prepared dry mix of crushed almonds and walnuts and coconut flour.

Vegetables and Herbs
1 carrot, peeled and grated
2 tbsp cucumber, finely chopped
¼ courgette (zucchini), chopped
3 baby sweetcorn, sliced
Handful of baby spinach, chopped
1 sprig fresh dill, to garnish

2 tbsp pearl barley

Dry Items
1 tbsp white hulled sesame seeds
1 tbsp pecan nuts
1 tbsp Polly's avian herbal tea – Nature Boost

DINNER
Barley Chop

First put the barley and water in a pot and bring to the boil. Reduce heat, cover and simmer until tender. Drain and let it cool down.

Chop all the vegetables as suggested and place them in a bowl.

Add all the dry items followed by the cooked barley, toss gently. Garnish with fresh dill.

SUNDAY

BREAKFAST
Parrot's Veggie Omelette (with mini side chop)

1 free-range egg
1 tbsp red bell pepper, finely chopped
1 tbsp broccoli, finely chopped
1 chilli pepper, chopped
1 tbsp raw peas
1 tbsp raw sweetcorn
1 tsp coriander seeds
1 tsp flaxseeds (linseeds)
1 tbsp organic raw coconut oil

Mini Side Chop
1 tbsp cucumber, finely chopped
1 tbsp spinach
1 tbsp carrot, grated
2 tbsp butternut squash, grated

Sprouted
1 tbsp milk thistle seeds

Melt the raw coconut oil in a frying pan over a very low heat.

Add the finely chopped pepper, broccoli, chillies, peas, sweetcorn and cook gently on low heat for about 5 min.

While the vegetables are cooking, beat the egg until frothy and add in the coriander and flaxseeds. Pour the egg mixture over the cooked vegetable evenly and allow to cook. When the base firms up, flip the omelette to the other side and cook it.

Leave it to cool down before serving to your bird. Place it on a plate if your bird is joining you for breakfast, or serve it in their bowl and add the mini chop on the side.

Tip: Cook the omelette on a very low heat so it won't burn. *Eggs to be fed sparingly – no more than once a month. Whites are the healthier part of the egg to be offered. Plant-based protein is always preferable to animal protein.*

44   A PARROT'S HEALTHY MEAL PLANNER

AFTERNOON SNACK
Summer Fruit Mix

Chop all the fruit as instructed and place it in your bird's favourite bowl, then add the dry items. Mix and serve.

Fruit
¼ red apple, diced
½ kiwi, diced
2 tbsp cantaloupe melon (with seeds), diced
1 tbsp papaya, with seeds
1 tbsp blueberries
¼ cup strawberries, chopped
1 tbsp raspberries, whole
1 tbsp gooseberries, cut in half
¼ orange, peeled and diced

Dry Items
1 tbsp organic dried hibiscus flowers
1 tbsp dried whole rosehips
1 tbsp almonds, crushed
1 tsp chia seeds

Nutritional Tip: It is advisable to only include chia seeds within moist food as dry chia seeds can cause crop blockage. They swell up and absorb about 10–12 times their weight when they are exposed to water.

¼ sweet potato, cut into chips
2 slices butternut squash
1 slice courgette (zucchini)
1 slice red bell pepper
1 leaf of black cabbage
1 tsp dried thyme
1 tbsp organic raw coconut oil
1 bamboo skewer

DINNER
Parrot's Healthy "Burger Meal"

Preheat the oven to 170 °C/350 °F. Cut the sweet potato into chunky chips then drizzle with melted raw coconut oil and sprinkle with thyme. Place onto parchment paper on a baking tray and bake for about 20 minutes. Don't worry if the chips aren't cooked thoroughly as your bird can eat them raw too but make sure the chips won't burn. Take them out of the oven and leave to cool.

Then peel the butternut squash and cut a couple of thin round slices or use a round cookie cutter. To assemble the burger, place one slice of the butternut squash (raw) at the bottom and layer all the other vegetables on top of each other and finish with the second slice of the butternut squash. To help hold the burger together, pierce it all the way through with a bamboo skewer. This can be great as a foraging meal with plenty to eat.

Tip: Always use fresh vegetables. You can add or substitute any of the ingredients as long as it fits into the bird's safe food category.

Safety Tip: Obtaining appropriate bird-safe cookware is essential and any Teflon pans should not be used around birds. Birds' complex respiratory systems and high metabolic rate make them extremely sensitive to airborne toxins. The safe choice to replace your Teflon pots and pans with is stainless steel, copper-clad stainless steel, copper, glass or cast iron.

VEGETABLE SMOOTHIES

Smoothies are easy to make, endlessly versatile, and you can sneak in those green nutritious goods while not worrying that your flock will turn up their beaks at something green. You can add seeds and chopped nuts to boost the nutrition and get them to forage for those delicious nuts. A piece of fruit will add that bit of sweetness to offset the taste of the greens. Vegetable smoothies are a great source of fibre, protein, and a whole host of vitamins, antioxidants and other nutrients! It's a great way to introduce healthy greens to a fussy parrot. Super easy, super refreshing.

Nutritional Tip: Smoothies made from fruit only are usually high in sugars as their natural sugars are being released from their cells during the blending process. We call these natural sugars "free sugars".

How to make a parrot smoothie

To make any of these smoothies, first roughly chop all the fruit and vegetables and simply place all the ingredients (except nuts) into a blender and blend until smooth. Add water if the consistency is too thick and then add chopped nuts or seeds. Use organic produce if possible. Always wash the fruit and vegetables thoroughly and peel the skin off where required, as some skin can still contain pesticide residue. You can always adjust ingredients and quantities as required. Smoothies can be refrigerated for up to 24 hours or turned into an ice lolly during hot summer days.

GREEN FIX
1 handful of kale
1–2 red apples, skinless and seedless
1 sprig of fresh mint
1 tsp chia seeds
1 tsp sunflower seeds (add at the end)
Water as needed

RED VELVET
1 handful of kale
½ beetroot, peeled
½ carrot, peeled
1 celery
1 tbsp fresh ginger
1 small pear
½ kiwi
1 tsp Brazil nuts, finely chopped
1 tbsp coconut flakes, to garnish
Water as needed

SUNSHINE SMOOTHIE
1 large carrot
¼ cup butternut squash
1 sprig of parsley
1 cup papaya (add the seeds too [once blended])
1 cup fresh cranberries
1 tsp flaxseeds
Pinch of Ceylon cinnamon
Water as needed

THE POWER SMOOTHIE
1 handful of spinach
1 cup purple kale
½ cup courgette
2 tbsp blueberries
1 tbsp blackberries
1 tsp black sesame seeds
1 tsp white sesame seeds, to garnish
Coconut water as needed

Nutritional Facts

Kale – known as green superfood that is rich in vitamins A, B6, C and K, and loaded with antioxidants. Supports digestion and detoxes the stomach.

Spinach – great source of vitamins A, C, E and K, which helps strengthen the immune system. Feed in moderation as it is high in oxalates.

Carrots – important root vegetable that should be part of your bird's diet. High in antioxidants as well as vitamin A, which is essential to a bird's immune system, kidneys, skin and feathers.

Ginger root – well known for its medicinal properties. This super powerful herb aids in reducing inflammation and supports digestion due to its specific fibre. In addition to its antifungal properties, it also helps to fight off bacterial infections.

Safety Tip: Avoid commercially produced coconut water that may be processed and contains sugar, preservatives or other components that could harm your bird. Always read the packaging labels. You can always buy a whole, raw coconut, crack it and drain the water out. The same applies to commercially produced smoothies. Be careful about offering fruit smoothies as they are little sugar bombs.

SHOPPING LIST

With our handy grocery list, we will make the shopping faster and easier for you. Simply photocopy and print these pages then take them with you when going to the shops. Items marked with * are optional to use. Remember, you can always substitute, remove, and expand on this to adjust it to your bird's taste and size.

Tip: Many of the dry items can be purchased in large packs or in bulk so they will definitely last you longer than just one week. Organic produce is preferred when possible.

Monday

VEGETABLES/HERBS
- Basil microgreens*
- Beetroot
- Black cabbage
- Brussels sprouts
- Butternut squash
- Carrot
- Fennel
- Fresh coriander
- Kohlrabi
- Pak choi
- Pumpkin or any type squash
- Red amaranth microgreens*
- Red bell pepper
- Sweetcorn

DRY ITEMS
- Almonds
- Cashews
- Chickpeas (garbanzo beans)
- Dried blueberries and cranberries
- Flaxseeds (linseeds)
- Hemp seeds
- Milk thistle seeds
- Organic coconut flakes (unsweetened)
- Organic coconut flour
- Organic rolled oats (unsweetened)
- Polly's avian herbal tea
- Pumpkin seeds (pepitas)
- Spray millet (for small beaks)*
- Sunflower seeds
- Tree nuts – hazelnuts, walnuts, macadamia nuts, almonds, Brazil nuts, cashews, pine nuts
- White hulled sesame seeds

OTHER
- Flaxseed oil*
- Pansy flowers*

Tuesday

VEGETABLES/HERBS
- Broccoli
- Butternut squash
- Carrot
- Cauliflower
- Courgette (zucchini)
- Cucumber
- Fresh rosemary
- Green beans
- Green chilli peppers
- Green pepper
- Kale
- Purple sprouting broccoli
- Red chilli peppers

DRY ITEMS
- Amaranth
- Black quinoa
- Black sesame seeds
- Chickpeas
- Ground flaxseeds (linseeds)
- Pearl barley
- Radish seeds
- Red lentils
- Walnuts
- Whole rosehips
- Yellow split peas

FRUIT
- Variety of seasonal fruit that is available in your country

OTHER
- Organic raw coconut oil*

Wednesday

VEGETABLES/HERBS
- ❏ Broccoli
- ❏ Brussels sprouts
- ❏ Carrot
- ❏ Fresh curly parsley
- ❏ Green beans
- ❏ Orange bell pepper
- ❏ Red bell pepper
- ❏ Red chilli pepper
- ❏ Red mustard microgreens
- ❏ Sugar snap peas
- ❏ Swiss chard

DRY ITEMS
- ❏ Barley flour
- ❏ Barley flakes
- ❏ Black sesame seeds
- ❏ Cashews
- ❏ Chia seeds
- ❏ Green lentils
- ❏ Hemp seeds
- ❏ Mung beans
- ❏ Organic coconut flakes (unsweetened)
- ❏ Organic rolled oats (unsweetened)
- ❏ Polly's avian herbal tea – Golden Blossom
- ❏ Pumpkin seeds (pepitas)
- ❏ Radish seeds
- ❏ White hulled sesame seeds

FRUIT
- ❏ Banana
- ❏ Blackberries
- ❏ Blueberries
- ❏ Green plantain
- ❏ Green plum
- ❏ Honeydew melon
- ❏ Pomegranate seeds
- ❏ Red apple

OTHER
- ❏ Live waxworms or mealworms
- ❏ Organic egg
- ❏ Organic raw coconut oil
- ❏ 1 pansy flower*
- ❏ Small bamboo skewers

Thursday

VEGETABLES/HERBS
- ❏ Baby peppers
- ❏ Baby spinach
- ❏ Beet microgreens*
- ❏ Butternut squash
- ❏ Cabbage microgreens*
- ❏ Carrot
- ❏ Courgette (zucchini)
- ❏ Cress microgreens
- ❏ Fresh mint
- ❏ Green beans
- ❏ Kale
- ❏ Kohlrabi
- ❏ Marrow squash
- ❏ Okras
- ❏ Purple sprouting broccoli
- ❏ Red bell pepper
- ❏ Savoy cabbage
- ❏ Sweetcorn
- ❏ Turnip
- ❏ White chicory

DRY ITEMS
- ❏ Almond flakes
- ❏ Almonds
- ❏ Brazil nuts
- ❏ Buckwheat
- ❏ Green lentils
- ❏ Hazelnuts
- ❏ Macadamia nuts
- ❏ Mung beans
- ❏ Pine nuts
- ❏ Polly's avian herbal tea – Golden Blossom
- ❏ Polly's avian herbal tea – Nature Boost
- ❏ Red quinoa

FRUIT
- ❏ Honeydew melon
- ❏ Pomegranate seeds
- ❏ Red apple
- ❏ Strawberries
- ❏ Watermelon

OTHER
- ❏ Ceylon cinnamon

Friday

VEGETABLES/HERBS
- ❑ Beetroot
- ❑ Carrot
- ❑ Cauliflower
- ❑ Chilli pepper
- ❑ Courgette (zucchini)
- ❑ Fresh curly parsley
- ❑ Kale
- ❑ Radish
- ❑ Raw peas
- ❑ Red chilli pepper
- ❑ Sugar snap peas
- ❑ Yellow and green bell peppers

DRY ITEMS
- ❑ Barley flakes
- ❑ Buckwheat
- ❑ Coriander seeds
- ❑ Fenugreek seeds
- ❑ Green lentils
- ❑ Kamut
- ❑ Milk thistle seeds
- ❑ Mung beans
- ❑ Organic brown rice
- ❑ Pearl barley
- ❑ Polly's avian herbal tea – Nature Boost*
- ❑ Radish seeds
- ❑ Your bird's seed mix

FRUIT
- ❑ Red apple

Saturday

VEGETABLES/HERBS
- ❑ Baby spinach
- ❑ Baby sweetcorn
- ❑ Bird's eye chillies
- ❑ Broccoli
- ❑ Buttonhole kale (purple)
- ❑ Carrot
- ❑ Courgette (zucchini)
- ❑ Cress microgreens
- ❑ Cucumber
- ❑ Fresh dill
- ❑ Fresh oregano
- ❑ Green beans
- ❑ Lamb's lettuces
- ❑ Okra
- ❑ Pumpkin
- ❑ Savoy cabbage
- ❑ Sweet potato
- ❑ White chicory
- ❑ Yellow and red bell peppers

DRY ITEMS
- ❑ Almonds
- ❑ Corn*
- ❑ Ground flaxseeds (linseeds)
- ❑ Milk thistle seeds
- ❑ Organic coconut flour
- ❑ Organic rolled oats (unsweetened)
- ❑ Pearl barley
- ❑ Pecan nuts
- ❑ Polly's avian herbal tea – Nature Boost
- ❑ Pumpkin seeds (pepitas)
- ❑ Shelled hemp seeds
- ❑ Walnuts
- ❑ White hulled sesame seeds

FRUIT
- ❑ Banana

Sunday

VEGETABLES/HERBS
- ❑ Black cabbage
- ❑ Broccoli
- ❑ Butternut squash
- ❑ Carrot
- ❑ Courgette (zucchini)
- ❑ Cucumber
- ❑ Chilli pepper
- ❑ Spinach
- ❑ Sweet potato
- ❑ Raw peas
- ❑ Raw sweetcorn
- ❑ Red bell pepper

DRY ITEMS
- ❑ Almonds
- ❑ Coriander seeds
- ❑ Chia seeds
- ❑ Dried thyme
- ❑ Dried whole rosehips
- ❑ Flaxseeds (linseeds)
- ❑ Milk thistle seeds
- ❑ Organic dried hibiscus flowers

FRUIT
- ❑ Blueberries
- ❑ Cantaloupe melon
- ❑ Gooseberries
- ❑ Kiwi
- ❑ Orange
- ❑ Papaya
- ❑ Raspberries
- ❑ Red apple
- ❑ Strawberries

OTHER
- ❑ Bamboo skewer
- ❑ Free-range egg
- ❑ Organic raw coconut oil

ABOUT THE AUTHOR

Karmen Budai

Karmen Budai started off with her successful book, *A Parrot's Fine Cuisine Cookbook and Nutritional Guide*, published in 2018. Her parrot's story was the main factor that prompted her to create her first cookbook for parrot owners and set her on the journey of helping other parrot owners struggling to feed their birds a healthy nutritional diet.

Her passion for parrots and their wellbeing then led her to the creation of this healthy parrot's meal planner to inspire other bird owners and help them on their journey with their bird diet transition. Karmen is originally from a small country in Europe called Slovakia. Since childhood, she had a creative streak, which led to studying fashion design in her college years. Fashion remained a hobby and she moved on to a career in the corporate environment. She moved to the United Kingdom in 2004, intending only to stay for a few years, but settled there with her family. She has the most demanding, feathered, velcro cockatoo, called Polly, that consumes the majority of the family's time. Polly is a toddler that will never grow up. There are also new additions to the family: four delightful budgies and an Indian Ringneck Parakeet, Rio, who's the family's little chatterbox.

Karmen Budai now runs her own online store for avian herbal tea provision, first in the UK and Europe, called Polly's Natural Parrot Boutique, which is another way of helping to provide enrichment to all birds and goes hand in hand with the message she's eager to share with all parrot owners.

ABOUT THE CONTRIBUTOR

Dr Stephanie Lamb

Stephanie Lamb, DVM, Dipl ABVP, has always desired to provide good health, happiness and care to all animals. She grew up in Las Vegas, NV, and after graduating from UNLV with a BS in Biology, she attended veterinary school at the University of Minnesota. Upon finishing veterinary school she performed a one-year internship in avian and exotic medicine followed by a two-year residency in avian medicine and surgery in Wilton, CT. After completing her residency, Dr Lamb worked in Southern California and Arizona at exotics-exclusive animal hospitals. During this time she gained extensive knowledge and became skilled in treating exotic mammals, birds, reptiles, amphibians and wildlife. During her career she has also worked with many humane societies, parrot and rabbit rescue groups, wildlife centres and raptor rehabilitation facilities.

She is always striving to learn more and is focused on contributing to the advancement of knowledge of avian and exotic animal medicine by providing the highest quality veterinary care possible. She and her husband share their home with dogs, geckos, fish, and 13 birds. Dr Lamb passed her Avian Medicine boards in the autumn of 2014.

She has publications in peer-reviewed journals about avian and exotic mammal medicine and has lectured at county, state and national veterinary conferences about avian medicine. She has also spoken to local bird, reptile and rabbit clubs in her community.

RESOURCES

Avian Herbal Teas
Unique avian herbal tea provisions in the UK and Europe.
We believe that by including avian herbal teas in your bird's diet you can enhance their quality of life.
- @pollysnaturalparrotboutique
- @pollysnaturalparrotboutique
- @pollysnaturalp1

www.pollysnaturalparrotboutique.com

Dr Stephanie Lamb, DVM, Dipl ABVP (Avian Practice)
www.azeah.com

World Parrot Trust
An international leader in science-based, results-oriented, parrot conservation and welfare efforts since 1989
- @WorldParrotTrust
- @ParrotTrust

www.parrots.org
Your kind donation will help to save parrots.
www.parrots.org/donate

Please join us at **www.pollysnaturalparrotboutique.com** to receive updates, giveaways and notifications of new products. If you would like to know more about advertising in Polly's future editions, please contact us at **info@pollysnaturalparrotboutique.com**

www.ingramcontent.com/pod-product-compliance
Lightning Source LLC
Chambersburg PA
CBHW061128070526
44584CB00033B/4262